# WE HONOUR AND REMEMBER OUR BRAVE SOLDIERS

Sharon Lake

Order this book online at www.trafford.com
or email orders@trafford.com

Most Trafford titles are also available at major online book retailers.

Printed in the United States of America.

ISBN: 978-1-4269-4995-1 (sc)
ISBN: 978-1-4269-4996-8 (e)

*Trafford rev.12/20/2010*

North America & international
toll-free: 1 888 232 4444 (USA & Canada)
phone: 250 383 6864 ✦ fax: 812 355 4082

## THESE POEMS,

I dedicate to all the brave soldiers.

## THESE POEMS ARE A TRIBUTE,

To all our proud Canadian military.
Who are serving around the world.
And making a difference,
Touching lives wherever they go.
Our past and our present.
Our young and old.
We remember them all.

# CONTENTS

# ABOUT THE AUTHOR:

Hi everyone, my name is Sharon Lake. I'm Canadian born; I came from a military family. I worked in the mess halls in Kingston Ontario, and Cold Lake, Alberta. I was preparing meals for our Soldier's morning, noon and, night. My military friends loved my poems. And said I should write my poetry for everyone to read. My other hobbies include drawing, painting, Needlepoint and cooking. I started to write these poems on August 21, 2009 and I hope you enjoy them, as much as I enjoyed writing them for you.

# GOD BLESS OUR TROOPS

God bless our Canadian and American Troops.
Our Brother's and our Sister's,
We keep each other safe in combat.
We pray for safe returns,
To our families.
You're in our thoughts, and our prayers,
Forever in our hearts always.
We love our soldier's.
And God Bless you all,
For proudly serving our Countries.
And keeping us safe.

# WHAT MAKES A SOLDIER?

Someone big, strong and brave.
Someone willing to serve their country,
Here and overseas.
Someone who's not afraid,
Of danger.
Someone who has the willpower,
To take on any job,
And make it there's.
Someone who's open,
And willing to listen.
Someone who's considered,
Takes it all to heart.
Someone willing to learn,
A new trade.
Someone to be a,
Proud Canadian Soldier.

# MILITARY LIFE

Military Life is not for
Everyone.
Military life is hard
Not knowing.
From day to day,
Where you're going to be.
Not able to see your family
For long periods of time.
What makes a military person
It takes a strong, brave, courageous,
And caring person.
Someone with a big heart,
Someone who's not afraid.
Of being away from their love ones
And who's Proud to Serve Their Country.
And were so proud of them,
For being them our Canadian soldiers.

# WHAT A CANADIAN SOLDIER FEELS...

Wanting to feel important,
Belonging to a proud family.
Wanting to make,
Something of myself.
Wanting my family,
To be proud of me.
Doing something,
I was trained for.
That I have,
A passion for.
Being everything,
I can be.
Being a proud,
Canadian Soldier.
And supporting,
My military family
All the way.

# BEHIND EVERY SOLDIER

Behind every Soldier,
Stands a proud family.
A family who believes in,
Their son, daughter, husband,
Wife, niece, or nephew, anyone.
Who wants to be a Soldier?
They stand and believe,
In their dreams.
They help make it run smoothly,
With being understanding.
There, there to cheer you up,
When you're down.
They believe in you every step,
Of the way.
They believe you will make
A great soldier.
Every step of the way,
As long as you have a proud, loving family,
Who believes in you,
And you believe in yourself.

# BEHIND A STRONG SOLDIER

Behind a strong Soldier,
Stands a wife.
Someone to hold the fort down,
And takes care of the young.
To explain to the kids,
Where dad has gone.
And letting them know,
We have to be strong.
We have to believe,
He won't be gone long.
We pray and keep the faith.
He will be home really soon,
So we can continue life the way we were.
Until the next time,
When we have to part.

# WE HAVE TO REMEMBER

We have to remember,
It's not only hard on the wives.
But it is extremely hard on the kids the not knowing.
Where have they gone?
Not realizing their mom or dad.
Made a pledge to their country,
They would go help whenever needed.
All the kids can do is pray,
And hope they come home really soon.
So they can continue life the way it was before they left.

# THE FACES BEHIND

The faces behind,
Every soldier can tell a story.
They would say they're proud of them,
And happy that they followed their dreams,
Every step of the way.
They didn't give up,
They stood their grounds.
Even when pushing came to shoving,
They didn't back down.
They wanted to become one of
Our proud Canadian Soldiers.
Having their family backing them,
Every step of the way.

# SOLDIER'S PRAYER

They pray to keep our Country safe,
To keep the peace,
To stand on guard for their Country.
To proudly serve overseas,
To be strong, brave, and courageous.
Able to lend an ear to a fellow Soldier.
Or just a shoulder to lean on.
Or just to be a good listener.
To protect,
To care.
To be proud to wear the uniform.
They pray to keep each other safe in combat.
To comfort a loved one, or a total stranger.
To be a proud Soldier.
To support their Country all the way.

# THIS POEM

Is for my Canadian and American,
Brothers and Sisters.
Serving in the military,
We all stand together,
Helping each other.
Through this war and previous wars.
We fight beside each other,
And we pray together.
And hope for safe returns,
For all of us.
To our families.

# ANGELS, ANGELS, ANGELS PLEASE KEEP OUR ANGELS.

Please keep our angels,
Our Canadian troops
In combat safe.
Our hard working,
Our brothers and our sisters.
And our military family safe.
In Gods arms,
And in our hearts,
And in our thoughts,
Every day we pray,
For a safe return to us.
And God Bless you all.
For proudly
Serving our Country.
And keeping us safe.

# OUR SOLDIER'S

Let us remember and honour,
All the proud Canadians.
Serving in our military,
Keeping the peace.
Let us remember,
Military life is hard.
And very dangerous.

# PLEASE KEEP

Please keep these,
Brave young soldiers safe.
Keep them out of harm's way.
Watch over them,
Every minute of the day,
To make sure there safe,
And out of harm's way.

# IT'S VERY STRESSFUL

Being a Soldier,
Or even a family of one.
The not knowing,
From day to day.
The uncertainty,
being ready to leave
At the drop of a dime,
Or with no notice.
Being proud to be a
Proud Canadian Soldier,
Every step of the way.
Just by following their dreams,
All the way.

# ARMY #1

**A** = Stands for all the Angels,
In our military.
**R**= Stands for reservist,
Being able to be call on,
When needed.
**M**= Stands for the men and women,
Proudly serving in our military.
**Y**= Stands for our young,
And our youthfulness.
Willing to proudly serve their Country,
Here and overseas.

# ARMY #2

**A**- Stands for Appreciate,
We appreciate everything
They're doing for us.
**R**- Stands for respect.
**M**-Stands for men and women,
Serving in our military.
**Y**- Stands for Young and
Courageous willing to serve,
Their country here and overseas,
Wherever needed.
Being a proud Canadian Soldier.
Making all of Canada proud,
That they're one of ours.
And we Love them all,
For being so brave.
We thank them for being them,
OUR CANADIAN SOLDIERS.

# HELICOPTER PILOTS

There all Angels,
In the sky high above
The ground.
Taking our soldiers,
From place to place.
Doing what they do best.
Transporting,
Our Canadian Soldiers,
In their wings of gold.
There known as,
Hero's in the clouds.

# MEDIC'S

**M**-Stands for Miracle workers,
In the military.
**E**-Stands for lots of Experience,
In their field of work.
**D**- Stands for Danger.
Dodging danger, day in, and day out.
That there away.
**I**- Stands for Independent.
Being able to work on their own.
**C**- Stands for Compassionate,
Very caring about their jobs.
**S**- Stands for Soldiers.
Proudly serving in our military.

# MESS COOK

**M**- Stands for Miracle Workers,
Who work in the Mess hall.
Planning your meals, morning,
Noon and night.
**E**- Stands for Experts,
In the kitchen.
**S**- Stands for service, with a smile.
**S**- Stands for Satisfy,
How we satisfy your taste buds.
**C**- Stands for a Cup of coffee,
We wish you would sit down
And have a chat with us.
**O**- Stands for Outstanding,
Were good at our jobs.
**O**- Stands for Oven,
We use to make your delicious
Meals up.
**K**- Stands for Kitchen,
Where we work,
Day and night.

# MESSHALL COOKS

**M**- Stands for Menus,
Planning your meals.
**E**- Stands for Experts.
**S**- Stands for Service.
**S**- Stands for Satisfy,
How we satisfy your taste buds.
**H**- Stands for Heavenly.
**A**-Stands for Angels, in the kitchen.
**L**- Stands for Loving spoonfuls.
**L**- Stands for Laughter.
**C**- Stands for Chefs, in training.
**O**- Stands for Outstanding.
**O**- Stands for Opportunity,
Knocks at our doors.
**K**- Stands for Kitchen,
Where we work day & night.
**S**- Stands for Smiles,
We greet you with morning,
Noon and night.

# MILITARY

**M**: Stands for men and women
Serving in our Military.
**I**:  Stands for Independence
**L**:  Stands for Loyal.
**I**:  Stands for Intelligent.
**T**:  Stands for Training.
**A**:  Stands for Army.
**R**: Stands for Reservist.
**Y**:  Stands for Young.

# NAVY

**N**-Stands for Navel,
**A**-Stands for Armour,
**V**-Stands for Vessel,
**Y**-Stands for Young, proud to serve our Country.

# RECRUIT

**R**- Stands for Ready,
To serve their country,
Here and overseas.
**E**- Stands for Exercise,
The training they do.
**C**- Stands for Caring.
**R**- Stands for Respect.
**U**- Stands for Uniform,
That they are proud to wear.
**I**- Stands for Interested,
How they can serve
Their country better.
**T**- Stands for Tactics,
And training.
How to move safely,
And out of harm's way.

# RESERVIST

**R**- Stands for Respect.
**E**- Stands for Exercise,
The training they do.
**S**- Stands for Service,
Serving in the military.
**E**- Stands for Eager,
To get the job done.
**R**- Stands for Ready,
To be called upon when needed.
**V**- Stands for Victory.
**I**- Stands for Independence,
**S**- Stands for Soldiers.
**T**- Stands for Tactics,
To plan their moves out.

# SOLDIERS

**S**- Stands for the sacrifices,
**O**-Stands Oath they give,
**L**-Stands for loyal,
**D**- Stands for dignity,
They honour and make it worthy.
**I**- Stands for Independent,
Being able to work on their own.
**E**- Stands for exercise,
The training they do.
**R**- Stands for retreat,
Go to a safe place.
**S**- Stands for safe,
And we pray they all come home,
 Safe to us.

# ANGELS, HERO'S, HERO'S, ANGELS #1

Whatever we call them.
They are all making a difference
In everything they are doing.
They're all someone's Child.
They are spreading their wings,
And leaving the nest.
And finding something
They love to do.
Finding something they have,
A passion for.
Making friends, seeing the sights,
Traveling around the world.
Touching lives wherever
They go.
Loving everything they do.
There also known as,
A proud Canadian Soldier.

# ANGELS, HERO'S HERO'S, ANGELS.

Whatever you call them,
There all Angels in our eyes.
There doing the work we can't,
But, they were trained to do.
They're brave, proud,
Canadian soldiers.
Making a big difference,
In everything they do.
Touching lives wherever
They go.
They are hero's in every way,
Every day.

# THESE ANGELS WERE MADE

To remember all the men and women,
Who have proudly served their country?
And who has kept us safe.
Through this war,
And previous wars.
We salute all these brave souls.
For giving their all,
In everything they do.
That's what makes them
Our angels.
For trying to keep the peace.
By putting their lives on the line.
We call them our Canadian Soldiers.

# WE SUPPORT OUR TROOPS

We support our Canadian Troops 100%,
All the way.
They're our brave,
Courageous soldiers every day.
These men and women,
Have GUTS.
And we believe in what,
They're doing.
And we believe in them,
All the way.

# OUR CANADIAN TROOPS

There all our Angels.
There trying to keep
The peace.
Making things run
Smoothly.
Sometimes there known,
As Hero's.
But, all the time there,
Known as Angels.
For everything,
They do.
And they need our support,
As Canadians.
To make the mission,
Run smoothly.
To let them know,
We care.

# HERO'S, ANGELS

Some call them Hero's,
Some call them Angels.
Whatever they are called
They're all Hero's,
To us.
There all brave,
And proud to be
A Soldier.
They're making a lot of,
Sacrifices for us.
Being away from there,
Loved ones.
For long periods,
Of time.
But, that's part of their jobs.
Proudly serving their Country,
Here and overseas.

# STAND UP

Stand up for our
Canadian Soldier's.
Show them we appreciate,
Everything they're doing.
Let them know we care.
And we support our
Canadian Soldier's
All the way.
They're our brave, proud,
Courageous men and women.
Serving in our military,
And our country.
Making a difference in
Everything they're doing.
Touching lives along the way.
Making changes for the better.
And we thank them.

# THEY SAY THERE'S ANGELS, AMONGST US

Well that's true.
These angels are proud,
Courageous, compassionate,
Strong, brave, caring,
Trusting and loving.
They're in every trade
And fields of the military.
We call them,
Our soldier's.
They're all proudly serving
Our country.
Here and overseas,
Wherever needed.
They're in our thoughts,
And our prayers.
And forever in our heart
Always.

# MEDIC'S

Compassionate Angels of Hope.
They're known as Miracle workers,
In the military.
With lots of experience,
In their field of work.
They take care of their own,
And others who are hurt.
They're very independent,
They're very compassionate,
About their work.
And very caring.
They take pride in their duties,
And their very sincere,
About their job.

# MY HEART GOES OUT

To our brave soldiers.
Who are in Afghanistan
Away from their loved ones,
This Christmas season
But there in our hearts,
Our thoughts in our prayers
Every day.
Wishing them all the best
This holiday season.
And always.

# THIS CHRISTMAS...

Let us remember
Our brave soldiers.
Our men and women serving,
Overseas and around the country.
Let us send them some
HOLIDAY cheer.
This is the loneliness time of the season.
Being away from their loved ones.
Seeing them smile on Christmas morning.
So that's why we can help,
With a little Christmas cheer
It goes a long way to these
Proud, brave Canadian and American Soldiers.
Who are always in our hearts,
And in our thoughts every day.

# ANGELS IN COMBAT

Please keep our Angels
In combat safe.
Our brave and our strong
Our courageous soldier's,
Safe and out of harm's way.
Watch over them,
And our military families every day.
They're in our hearts,
And our thoughts,
Every day.
We Pray,
For a safe returns,
To us.
And God Bless
You all.
For Proudly
Serving our Countries.
And keeping
Us safe.

# WHEN DUTY CALLS

When duty calls them,
Our Canadian Soldier's,
Jump into action.
Ready to serve their country,
Here and overseas,
Wherever needed.
Because they're our,
Proud Canadian Soldier's.
They will do anything,
For their Country.

# THERE'S ANGELS AMONGST US.

They're called,
Our Canadian Soldiers.
Our brave, strong,
Courageous, caring Soldiers.
Willing to proudly serve
Their Country.
Any way they can.
They're responsible,
Take any job serious.
Our Soldiers can be trusted,
With anything.
Our Soldiers put their lives in
Danger everyday there away.
And we thank them all,
For being so brave.

# CANADIAN SOLDIER'S PRAYER

They pray to keep our Country safe,
To keep the peace.
To stand on guard for their Country.
To proudly serve overseas.
To be strong, brave, and courageous.
Able to lend an ear to a fellow soldier.
Or a shoulder.
Or just to be a good listener.
To protect,
To care,
To proudly wear the uniform.
They pray to keep their Brother's and
Sister's safe in combat.
To comfort a loved one,
Or a stranger.
To be a proud Canadian Soldier,
All the way.

# THIS ANGEL, WAS MADE TO REMEMBER...

Our past and our present,
Our proud, brave, young,
And old soldiers.
We remember the sacrifice they,
Made for us.
And were so proud of them,
For making our country safe.

# THIS ANGEL WAS MADE, TO SHOW OUR SUPPORT...

To all the brave men and women,
Who are proudly serving our country.
And to all the men and women,
Who have proudly served their country?
The past and the present,
We remember them all.
By wearing this little angel,
In red.
Too thank them all.

# <u>VIMY RIDGE</u>

These brave young men,
Left their young brides,
And families behind.
To go fight a battle,
To support their country.
They gave the Ultimate Sacrifice,
For us 93 years ago.
By giving there all,
In everything they did.
They will always be
Known as a Hero,
And always in our hearts forever.
We will always remember
Them.
For our Freedom.
And thank them,
For being so brave.

# <u>WE HONOR AND REMEMBER</u>

Our brave Canadian Soldiers.
Who gave the ultimate sacrifice
For us 93 years ago.
At Vimy Ridge.
They were our young soldiers.
Leaving their young brides
And young families behind.
To go fight the battle,
For our Freedom.
A lot gave everything for us.
We will always remember,
And never forget these brave,
Courageous, strong men and women.
Who proudly served our country.
We thank them for everything,
They did for us.
And they will live in our hearts
Forever.

# VETERANS- NOWHERE IN THIS WORLD

Nowhere in this world,
Could I ever find or buy.
A great bunch
Of Veteran's.
Who proudly served?
Our country.
Our young our old,
Our past or present
We remember them all.
We appreciate everything
They did for us.
And we thank them,
For being so brave.
They showered us with kindness and love.
And sprinkled others too.
They're always in our thoughts,
And our prayers. And forever in
Our hearts always.

# VETERANS

Take the time out,
Listen to a veteran,
Listen to their stories.
Listen to what they
Endure suffer bravely,
Not complaining.
They proudly served,
Our Country.
And kept us safe.
They're our brave, courageous,
Proud veterans.
And we Love them all.
We remembered the,
Sacrifices these brave,
Men and women made for
Our Country.
And we thank them all,
For being so brave.

# PLEASE KEEP OUR VETERANS SAFE

Angels, angels,
Please keep our veterans safe.
Watch over them every minute of the day.
To make sure their safe, and out of harm's way.
These brave, proud, courageous.
Veterans proudly served our country.
Touched many hearts along the way.
Made a lot of sacrifices for our freedom.
Suffer bravely without complaining.
For our country. Saw a lot of their buddies,
Hurting or even dying. They watched in horror.
It's an image they can't erase from their memories.
The pain they carry with them all the time.
They remember the sacrifices. They made together.
Remembering the proud, brave,
Courageous men and women.
Who didn't come home, with them.
They will always remember.
And they will always be in our hearts forever.
We thank them.

# A GREAT BUNCH OF VETERANS

Nowhere in this world,
Could I ever find or buy,
A great bunch of Veteran's.
Who gave the Ultimate sacrifice,
For our Freedom.
We appreciate everything,
They did for our country,
And we thank them.
They showered us with,
Love and courage.
And sprinkled others too.
They're always in our thoughts,
And our prayers.
And forever in our
Hearts always.
We thank them all,
For being so brave.

# ANGELS, ANGELS, ANGELS PLEASE KEEP OUR BIG STRONG

Please keep our big, strong,
Courageous Canadian Soldier's,
Safe and out of harm's way.
God Bless you all,
For proudly serving our Country.
And keeping us safe,
Here and overseas.
You're in our thoughts,
And our prayers, and forever in our hearts.
Were sending you this message,
To let you know we Love you.
And were proud to stand beside you,
Because we believe in everything.
You're doing for our Country,
And we thank-you.
And pray for safe returns to us.
And God Bless you all.

# NOWHERE IN THIS WORLD

Could I ever find or buy.
A great bunch of
Mess cooks.
To hang out with.
We satisfy your taste buds,
With great food.
And we greet you morning,
Noon and night with a smile.
We shower you with laughter,
And sprinkle others too.
But, we certainly know,
How to clear a mess hall.
We just serve our meatloaf.
And everyone leaves.

# ANGELS, ANGELS, PLEASE KEEP OUR MEDICS

In combat safe.
Our hard working,
Brothers and sisters,
And our military family,
Safe in God's arms.
And our hearts,
And our thoughts,
And our prayers.
And God Bless you all,
For proudly serving
Our Country.
And keeping us safe.

# WE MET TOO YOUNG

For our hearts,
To beat as one.
You were leaving,
To go to war.
My heart was breaking inside.
Dreaming and wishing,
You didn't have to leave.
But, I knew it was your duty.
To serve and protect your country.
As a proud Soldier,
As you are to me.

# HERO'S

These Hero's had a dream.
They followed their dreams to the end.
They enjoyed,
And loved what they were doing.
They were all someone's, child.
They will always be, remembered.
In our thoughts, and our prayers.
They will always,
Live on in our hearts.
And our memories,
They will never be forgotten.
They believed in their dreams, they had,
And they will be missed forever.

# ANGELS, ANGELS, ANGELS PLEASE KEEP THESE BRAVE

Please keep these brave,
Courageous men and women
Safe and out of harm's way.
Keep our military family safe.
Let them know we Love them.
And we pray for safe returns
To their families.
There in our hearts, thoughts,
And our prayers.
We appreciate everything there doing,
For our Country.
And we say Thank-you,
To a great bunch of
Canadian Soldier's.
For making a difference in
Everything there doing.
And God Bless you all.

# THIS REMEMBRANCE DAY

Let us remember our fallen soldiers,
Our young and our old,
Our past and our present soldiers.
Let's take the timeout.
To remember the sacrifices,
These soldiers made.
The brave and courageous,
Men and women.
Who proudly serving
In our military,
We salute them all.
And thank them.

# THESE ANGELS WERE MADE TO REMEMBER OUR FALLEN SOLDIER'S

Remember their dreams,
Of being one of our great,
Canadian Soldier's.
Making a difference in what they were doing.
Believing in their dreams,
Believing in their mission.
Believing.
We salute them all
For being so brave.
They will always live on.
In our memories.
They will never be forgotten.
There one of our Angels now,
And always.

# HEADING OFF TO WAR

These brave young soldier's,
Were heading off to war,
The sad goodbyes,
To their loved-ones,
The hugs & kisses,
The tears rolling down their faces,
The picture they hold close,
To their hearts,
Praying they will return,
To hold and see them once again.
Off they ran by the hundreds& thousands.
Grabbing their helmet in one hand,
And their duffle bag and rifle in the other.
Running as fast as they could,
To catch up to the pack.
Jumping on the planes and choppers,
That awaited them,
To take them to the battlefields,
Where their lives would change forever.

# HEADING OFF TO WAR  - CONTINUES

Off they ran,
One by one,
To a destination unknown to them.
The uncertainty, the not knowing,
What they stepped into.
Worrying and wondering,
They're fears were getting the best of them.
Praying they could move forward,
One step at a time.
Stepping on the unknown soil,
Where their lives would change,
Forever.
Witnessing the pain, the hurt,
The screaming children.

# HEADING OFF TO WAR -CONTINUED

They watched in horror,
Watching their buddies being shot,
And seeing them even dying,
In front of them,
It's an image they can't erase from their memories.
The memories will stay with them forever.
Now our soldier's,
Are trying to face life again,
Like it was before,
They left.
But it will never be the same ever again.

# THEY LEFT #1

They left much too young,
To go on a far away journey.
To see the world and the sights,
To experience life a different way,
To follow their comrades into the fields.
Where they would experience life,
Through a whole new way.
That they would never forget.
The hurt the pain,
That they would have to carry
With them always to the end.
The lost the pain would be too much,
To handle for some.
And they live in us always
And forever in our hearts.
The sacrifices they made.
Will always be with us,
They were one of us,
And will stay with us always.
Till the end.

# THEY LEFT   THEY LEFT #2

They left so young,
And came back all grown-up.
They saw the world a different way,
Through the fights and battles.
They lost a lot of their friends,
Their lives will be changed forever.
They're hearts will always remember,
they will never forget their friends.
They will always carry the pain,
With them till the end.
When they can be together again.

# THE MISSION

The phone rang
It was my Sir.
Telling me we were,
Going to bug out.
Telling me to grab my bags, and my gear.
Telling me to go to the airport,
And getting my order papers.
Because I was leaving,
On a far away journey.
The only thing I was allowed to do
Was say good-bye to my loved ones.
The hugs the kisses the tears,
Rolling down our faces,
And the parting kiss,
Was all we could do.
The picture I hold close to my heart,
Of my loved ones.
Praying I will return to see,
Them again.
And not just a memory of me.

# THE FIRING

The firing started again,
There was no place to run
So I jumped into the bunker,
With my friends.
And prayed we would be safe,
But the firing got closer.
We had to dig out quickly
Or we too would be gone.
But we manage to hide from the shelling.
But many of our friends,
Didn't make it out.
So we think of them every
Remembrance Day.
There in our hearts and our prays every day.
We remember the sacrifices they made for us.
There one of our brave soldiers.
Who gave everything for us.
And we thank them all.
They will never be forgotten.

# EMOTIONS ON THE FRONT LINE

My heart is racing; I'm in a cold sweat,
I'm trembling; I can't catch my breath,
I'm praying my buddies are safe.
Hoping I can catch up to them,
They seem so far away.
Wishing I could reach out and grab one,
So I could feel a little safer.
Dodging the shelling and the explosions,
My legs are a little shaky. Wondering if,
I will make it to them,
My emotions are running wild,
I can't think straight.
I'm scared,
Wishing I was somewhere safe.

# BATTLEFIELD SCARS

The emotions,
A Canadian soldier carry,
Through thick and thin of it.
The hurt the pain, the nightmares,
Cold sweats, heart racing.
The jumpiness. Being Alert, all the time.
Unable to think straight.
Praying they could forget,
So they can carry on with life.
The way they remembered it
But it will never be the same again.
The hurt the pain, the lost of their buddies.
The memories that will haunt them.
Unable to sleep,
Because of the nightmares,
Listening to all the loud noises in my head.
Wishing they would stop.
My heart is racing and coming into my throat.
Wishing all these fears would come to a end.
So I could sleep once again.

# <u>SOLDIERS</u>

Our brave Canadian Soldiers,
Face a lot in their lifetimes.
Our men and women,
Come back with the pain,
Locked up inside them.
Wishing they could forget.
None of us will ever know,
What they went through,
Unless we were there with them.
Now they're trying to face
Life again.

# THE HURT THE PAIN

The emotions running,
Through my blood.
The pain the suffering,
My heart aching in pain.
Wondering how I will move on,
With life.
How will I stop the nightmares?
The screaming.
Seeing the children in pain,
Wishing I can take the pain away.
And hold them.
But, these feelings don't stop,
For no one.
They're with us all the time.
It's an experience, in life.
We won't forget.
They will always be with us
Always.
Until the end.

# OUR SOLDIER'S

Conquer all types of fears,
Everyday there away.
They face them straight on.
It takes a strong person,
To overcome their fears.
Overcome what they faced,
Every day they were away.
They saw pain.
They seen killing.
They seen children hurting
And wished they could stop the pain.
They saw their buddies hurting.
And prayed it would all come to an end.
So they could carry on.
Without the pain.

# EMOTIONS

These men and women,
Face a lot in their lifetime.
But, a lot come back with the pain,
Locked up inside them.
Wondering how to let go.
To stop the suffering inside of them,
So they can carry on with life,
The way they remembered it.
But that's not easy for them,
To let go of the pain the hurt.
All the feelings running wild through their blood,
Trying to calm down, trying to relax.
Trying to remember the good times they had.
For that, there all gone it's just a memory washed away.

# THE LOST

My heart breaks,
Every time I hear we have
Lost another brave Canadian
Soldier.
But, my heart also breaks for,
You guys.
Watching your fellow soldier,
Die to this War.
Remembering all the good times,
You shared with your buddy.
And remembering all your plans,
After this mission.
That you promise to do together.
But, now you have all this pain,
In your heart, instead.
Now you have a long road to recovering,
Remembering your buddy as a Hero.
And holding all those memories,
You made together.
Close to your heart forever.

# WEAR THIS LITTLE ANGEL

To show your support.
To our military,
And their families.
Just wearing this,
Little red Angel.
Shows you care.
You care for our brave,
Proud Canadian Soldiers.
Who are proudly serving,
Our Country.
For that we wear,
This little Angel.
To say Thank-you.

# YOU NEVER LEAVE

Your military family,
They're always there
In your heart.
Wherever you go,
You think of them,
Day and night,
And pray there all safe.
So you can keep them,
Close to your heart always.
They're always in your thoughts,
And your prayers.
Forever in your heart,
Till the end.

# <u>MY HEART BREAKS</u>

My heart breaks every time,
I hear we have lost another
Young soldier to this war.
For this, this little Angel,
Brings this prayer too you.
This little Angel is here,
For support.
She holds a special memory,
In her heart for you.
To keep your memories alive.

# THE MILITARY FAMILY

The military family,
We all feel the pain.
When we lose one of our family,
Members to this war.
There one of our brave, proud,
Canadian soldiers.
Who are trying to keep us safe.
By putting their life in harm's way.
For that we all thank them
For being so brave.

# OUR TEARS FLOW#1

Our hearts ache in pain.
Every time we lose one,
We all feel the pain.
We are all sadden to hear,
About another soldier gone
Today.
It's another sad day,
For Canada.

# THERE ONE OF OUR BRAVE

There one of our brave
Proud Canadian Soldiers
They will live on,
In our hearts.
We will never forget them
Their one of us.
They were our young,
Proud Canadian Soldier's.
They will live on forever.
They made a difference,
Touched so many lives.
They will always be
Remembered.

# OUR CANADIAN SOLDIER'S

There one of our Angels.
They will live on,
In our thoughts,
And our prayers every day.
We wish their families
The best of luck.
We will always honour,
Their son, brother, husband,
Father, uncle and friend.
Because they were one of our,
Proud Canadian Soldier's.
We will remember them always.
Till the end when we meet again.

# AS PROUD CANADIANS

As proud Canadians,
We feel the pain.
When we lose another soldier
To this war.
Our hearts aches in pain
Our tears flow.
We pray this war,
Will come to an end.
So we can bring,
Our troops home safe.
So we don't feel,
This pain anymore.
So we can keep our,
Young and old safe.
In our hearts
Forever.

# THIS LITTLE ANGEL

This little Angel,
Holds a special place
In her heart for you.
For your pain and sorrow,
And to tell you.
Someone loves you.
In this dark time
Of your life.
Remember all of those,
Memories you hold so
Dear and close to your heart.

# __MY HEART ACHES__

My heart aches,
For the Fallen Soldiers Family.
They were one of our proud,
Canadian Soldiers.
Proudly serving their country,
Trying to keep the peace.
We will always remember them,
In our thoughts and prayers every day.
They will never be forgotten,
Cause they were someone's, child.
They will always be remembered,
Because they were doing something,
They believed in.
They were following their dreams.

# OUR HEARTBREAKING IN PAIN

Our heartbreaking in pain,
Every time we hear,
We lost another Proud,
Canadian Soldier.
Who believed in their dreams.
Made a difference in what they
Were doing.
They will always be remembered,
For being so brave.
And for following their hearts,
In what they believed in.
We will always remember them,
In our thoughts and our prayers
Every day.
We think of what they did,
and how they changed things.
They will always be remembered,
As an Angel.
In our hearts forever.

# OUR TEARS FLOW#2

Our tears flow,
Our hearts ache in pain.
Every time we lose one,
We're all sadden to hear,
Another proud Canadian
Soldier gone today.
It's another sad day,
For our military family,
And all of Canada.
They're in our thoughts,
And our prayers,
Forever in our hearts
Always.

# MY HEART IS BREAKING

My heart is breaking,
My tears are flowing.
I am very sad for the family,
Of the latest fallen Soldier.
They were one of our,
Proud Canadian Soldiers.
We will always honour,
And remember their loved one.
As one of our brave, courageous,
Proud Soldiers.
They will always be in our thoughts,
And in our prayers.
Forever in our hearts.
We will always remember,
Them as our Angel.
Who proudly, served our Country.
And touched so many lives,
Along the way.
We thank them.

# IT'S ANOTHER SAD DAY

It's another sad day,
For our military family.
Having to say good-bye
To another family member.
Remembering them as one of our,
Brave, proud, and courageous, caring Soldier.
Touching lives wherever they went.
They will always be remembered,
As one of our Angels.
Now and always.
Always in our thoughts,
And our prayers.
And always in our hearts forever.
We will always remember them,
As one of our proud, Canadian Soldier's.
Who gave everything for us.
We will always keep their
Memories alive.
They will always be in our
HEARTS FOREVER.

# MY CONDOLENCE

My Condolence,
Goes to the family,
Of the latest fallen Soldier.
They were one of our,
Proud, brave, courageous,
Canadian Soldiers.
They touched so many lives,
Along the way.
They will be greatly missed,
Forever in our hearts,
Now and always.
We will always honour,
And remember them.
As one of our Proud,
Canadian Soldiers.
And remember everything,
They did for us.

# THIS LITTLE ANGEL

This little Angel,
Is here
My heart is breaking
In your time of grieve,
To express your sorrow
And your pain.
To show you there's
Light at the end.
The memories are always there.
You just have to remember,
And hold them close to you.
Hold them close to your heart,
Never let go.
Till the end,
When we meet again.

# REMEMBER, WE REMEMBER

We remember,
They believed in their dreams.
They gave their life,
By living their dreams,
And by believing in them
In loving what they were doing,
Making a difference
And touching lives,
Wherever they went,
They will always be remembered,
By what they did.
They will always be in our,
Thoughts and our prayers every day.
We believe in what they were doing,
They will always be an Angel in our heart.
Because they believed in them,
And we believe in them too.
We call them,
Our proud soldiers.

# MEDICS

They're our Angels
Of Hope.
Our Medic's are very
Compassionate.
They're known as our
Miracle workers
In the military.
Our Angels of hope,
Are very caring, loving,
Brave, strong and courageous.
They take pride in everything,
They're doing.
They're our proud,
Angels of Hope
And we love them all.
We thank them,
For being so brave.

# ANGELS, ANGELS, PLEASE KEEP OUR CANADIAN SOLDIER'S SAFE

Please keep our Canadian soldier safe,
And out of harm's way,
Watch over them every minute of the day,
To make sure there safe,
And out of harm's way.
There in our hearts,
And our thoughts every day.
We pray for a safe return to us
And God Bless you all,
For proudly serving our Country,
And keeping us safe.

# THE HOMECOMING

They were finally coming home.
The joy, the excitement, happiness, the tears realizing it was over.
Our Soldier's were finally coming home to their loved ones.
Waiting and watching for the planes to land.
Wondering why it was taking so long.
Our excitement was building and we couldn't contain our happiness.
Our tears were rolling down our faces.
Then finally it was getting louder,
Louder the kids were screaming and crying.
That's when we knew the planes had landed.
That's when we realized they were home, they were really here.
All of the sudden they're love-ones were running towards them.
The hugs, the kisses the tears running down their faces.
And feeling the calmness of realizing they were home.
Now they could catch up on precious time missed.
And make new memories together.
Remembering their friend, as a Hero,
They're in our thoughts, our prayers and forever in our hearts always.
They will never be forgotten.
They were one of us, and will stay with us always.

I just wanted to let our Soldiers know we appreciate everything they're doing for our country, to let them know we care. That's why I wrote this book of poetry about our soldiers. To let them know they're in our thoughts, and our prayers, and forever in our hearts always. This book is for anyone who loves our Soldier's. Our past and our present Soldier's we remember them all. And we thank them all, for being so brave.